Dissatisfaction
Between
Black and White

By
Elijah Muhammad
Messenger of Allah

Edited by
Nasir Hakim
**Founder, Messenger Elijah Muhammad
Propagation Society**

Dissatisfaction Between Black and White

By
Elijah Muhammad
Messenger of Allah

Edited by
Nasir Hakim
Founder, MEMPS

Published by
Secretarius MEMPS Publications
5025 N Central Avenue #415
Phoenix, Arizona 85012
Phone & Fax 602 466-7347
Email: secretariusmemps@cox.net
Web: www.memps.com

Printed in the United States of America

ISBN10# 1448630827
EAN13 9781448630820

Dedication

Dedicated
to my wife Rose,
the Believers
And Followers of
Elijah Muhammad,
Messenger of Allah.

Contents

Dedication iv

Preface and Introduction............................vii

Dissatisfaction Between Black and White 1

Persecution of The Righteous 5

One Hundred Percent Dissatisfied................. 13

A People Spoiled and Robbed 17

The Worst Robbery of All Time 19

Dissatisfaction: Something Must Be Done 23

Uncle Toms Worst Enemy To People............. 27

Allah (God) Offers You The Kingdom............. 31

Allah's Promise of Beneficence and Protection 35

A Mighty Great Kingdom Is On The Way........ 37

Unity Is Key For The Blackman 38

Short History of The Cause of Dissatisfaction 41

White Race's Identity Exposed....................... 45

Whites Are Natural Peace Breaker................. 47

We Can Not Live In Peace 50

The Filth That Filth Produces 53

The Shame of Integration 59

What is Islam, Christian and Muslim 61

A Prey Among Wolves................................... 65

War Within And War Without....................... 67

Educate Your Own Children.......................... 73

White Race Are The Murderers of Prophets.... 75

Prepare Yourself For The Day of Want............77

Respect of Intelligence and Authority 79

Do For Self or Suffer 83

Friendship In All Walks of Life 85

As Thou Has Done..86

My Record of Peace.......................................89

Appeal To The Intellectual and Professional Classes..91

Preface and Introduction

The climate, in 1967 America, was one of racial turbulence. America was at war from without, Vietnam and every place else the CIA was hard at work, and from within with its freed slaves. The once freed, so-called Negroes were on the move with excitement as a result of one of the oldest questions that plagued them as a people: shall they stay with whites and seek civil rights, with Martin Luther King, Jr. as the leading government sponsored spokesman or shall they seek human rights in a separate state or territory of their own, with God missioned, Messenger Elijah Muhammad?

The Reverend Dr. Martin Luther King, Jr., was all but ordained a second time, and the poster boy by the integrationist movement by the time he "won" the Nobel Peace Prize and his march on Washington. If anyone wanted an alternative to any form of separation from America, or any form of nationalism, then Martin was their man. He was a politically correct alternative to Elijah Muhammad.

It was not uncommon to see Negroes getting their heads beat in by police, hosed down by water cannons, bitten in the private parts and breast by vicious dogs or to even catch a quick glimpse on TV of the remains of an Negro children being pulled from a burned car, church or the covered head of an elementary school, Negro, female rape victim. To have witnessed these acts of carnage would make the average person weep and want to fight, or at least remove themselves from the place where they are being subjected to such treatment.

Yet, having been slaves in America for over 300 years and being completely robbed of the right to even know they we were human and the knowledge of what comes with it as a "natural" right, the so-called American once slave was trying to make good on an idea of integration. Not knowing that the idea was being force into their minds through media and other government sponsored forms of communication, many of them believed that they could live side by side with whites, while others of this frame of mind actually went so far as call themselves the brothers of whites. These were the words of the Reverend Martin Luther King, Jr.. He said that he didn't want to be a brother-in-law, but a real brother. Being proclaimed a civil rights leader by the establishment, he was the main vehicle by which thousands of other Negroes in America allowed themselves to be brutalized day in and day out for a dream that's as possible as a lamb laying down with or marrying a wolf. The wolf gets the prey and the lambs get a never fulfilled promise.

It seemed that regardless of the Negro being subjected to murder, lynching, rapes, robbery and many other heinous acts too numerous to list in this short introduction, at the hands of their former slave-master and their children, they still were willing to "turn the other cheek" and give the old slave master a pass. Why? It was in exchange for him taking off his horns, tail and laying down his pitch fork. They believed that the offer of integration was a satisfactory exchange. Yet, something was wrong. The conditions had changed.

There was another message coming from the slave quarters which the slave owners had not sanctioned nor authorized. There was another message that slipped in under the cover of darkness while men slept. There was another message that crept in like a thief in the night. There was another message that came to the slaves like the messages that were promised in the past to those who were promised a message. Elijah Muhammad said he received a message from God that was for the Blackman.

Elijah Muhammad knew the slave master and their children oh so well, being that he was from the south. After the civil war, in which foreign powers along with their Northern, New England proxies, virtually destroyed the south and cooped the North. With many Southerners eating out of trash cans in the aftermath of the civil war, the great migration of once-slaves migrated to the North in search of economic relief. Elijah Muhammad and his family just happened to be part of that course of history. After moving to Detroit and meeting Master Fard Muhammad, the rest is history and can be read in detail at www.memps.com, but for the sake of this writing, he received a message that would change history, the so-called Negroes future, and the American landscape forever.

This book delves into the counter position put forth by Elijah Muhammad as opposed to the offer sponsored by America for her once slaves. Messenger Elijah Muhammad made it known on the back of the Muhammad Speaks newspaper that, "We believe the offer of integration is hypocritical and is made by those who are trying to deceived the black people into believing that their 400 year old open enemy of freedom, justice and equality are, all of a sudden, their "friends." Furthermore, we believe that such deception is intended to prevent black people from realizing that their time in history has arrived for the separation from the whites of this nation. If the white people are truthful about their profess friendship toward the so-called Negro, they can prove it by dividing up America with their slaves.

Given, to date, that America has not demonstrated this proof, despite the dog and pony show of the last national election, dissatisfaction between black and white is just as real and vicious today as it was at the time of this speech by Elijah Muhammad, given in Phoenix, Arizona, 1967.

In this new age of globalization and the powerful affects of the internet, more and more it appears that the so-called Negroes condition is becoming more and more minute and obsolete. Messenger Elijah Muhammad still makes his case.

Dissatisfaction Between Black and White

xiv Dissatisfaction Between Black and White

Dissatisfaction Between Black and White

Phoenix, Arizona 1967

As-Salaam-Alaikum

In the Name of Allah, the most Merciful, to Whom all Holy Praise is due, the Lord of the Worlds, the most Merciful, Master of the day of judgment, in which we now live. I thank Thee, Oh Allah, in the Name of Master Fard Muhammad, for our meeting here this afternoon.

I and the brothers and sisters would like to thank the Mayor and Police of Phoenix for the opportunity to speak here in their beautiful building. I'm thankful that you meet here or anywhere to hear our voice, we're thankful. We want to be as a friend of them, not enemies. We want to live in peace with the people of sin, not in war. We want to show the people of sin that Muslims are not aggressive. We want to show the people of sin that we didn't come to Phoenix with aggressive intentions. We want Phoenix to know that we are from God and not from the devil. The devil has never have kept peace anywhere that he's went. We want Phoenix to know that we are not here trying to boast of nothing but the truth. We are not teaching anything but the truth. We teach the truth and carry it into practice.

When we first moved to Phoenix, we had a very hard time trying to get settled in peace. I want to thank you, although you probably have got tired of starting trouble, but we are here today to say that we don't intend to start any trouble. For we cannot be examples of righteous and the examples of peace, while rolling up and down the streets with a 45 caliber gun in our pocket, or walking the streets with a knife, provoking people to come out to fight. We are not here for that. This is not the way of Islamic people. We are people who want peace. We will fight if attacked, because this is the law of nature. But, I want you to remember this, my neighbors of peace, that Elijah Muhammad did not buy a home here to start trouble with you. If there is any trouble, you will have to start it. By nature, I am born of God, and by nature, I seek peace. By nature I am after righteousness, because by nature, I was born of the righteous.

I thank my brothers here; I'm quite sure you enjoyed them. Our brother, Muhammad Ali, who's here, told us that he went all over the earth preaching. He is the man that proclaims that he is the boxing champ; so, they come to a man that proclaims he is the best; not that he wanted to make it his work or profession, but he wanted to be just what he is, a minister of righteousness. He wanted to help me pull our people out of the fire. Oh yes, it's burning, don't worry.

I want to thank all of you visitors who are out there visiting us in this meeting this afternoon. Wherever you are from, I want you to know that we thank you for your presence. After we are through, if you feel like you would like to have a word to say to us about what you think of our religion, or what you think of us, or what you think of yourselves, that's entirely up to you. We will give you a chance to do so, but the time will be limited.

We want to again thank Allah for bringing to us our followers from the Mid-West, the East Coast and from the West Coast. We have around a thousand or more wise followers in the city, at least here in the state. It is not all of our followers now, I forbid them to waste their money coming far out here in Phoenix to probably not even see over a hundreds of people from Phoenix come out. We are already aware of these things. Yet, if there is only one, we would like to see that one, and we are thankful to Allah for bringing them safely through the trails of the highway, the planes of the air, and other dangers. We thank Allah for bringing them here safely.

Persecution of The Righteous

Again brothers, sisters and friends alike, I would like to sum up a few things here before we get done with our subject. As the minister touched upon, that we, the children of God, agreed to do this work; yet, for 37 years, I have been trying to get the truth over to my people. I ran from my people and other than my people for 7 years. I went hungry and out of doors to be here today. I suffered those seven years, just running, dodging from my own people who were out to kill me for a little sum of money, around $500 dollars from a fellow in Detroit, Michigan, who said he would get him a pack of rice and eat one grain a day until he could see that I was dead. So, he's dead now. I ran for 7 years going in and out of the congressional library almost daily, to hide around in there to study, reading books on Islam and Muhammad of 14,000 years ago. That is the way I spent a lot of my time.

I roomed with poor people and I roomed with the wealthy people. I wanted to learn both classes. After that, I was arrested by the FBI in Washington D.C. on the fifth month, on the eighth day of 1942. They took me to their jail, but first to their office and questioned me all night long until around 8 or 9 o'clock that morning, Saturday morning. It was on Friday when I was arrested. They sent a doctor to come down to examine me, to see if whether I was getting a little "off," but I still was standing humble. There was much said that night and there were many questions asked; mostly all were answered. After that, they sentenced me to five years. They call it a correctional institution, but we call it a little minor penitentiary. I spent time there for about three years and four or five months, in Milan Michigan. I also stayed in jail in Chicago, around ten or eleven months. I spent two months and fifteen days in Washington D.C. before they ever came down to say if whether or not they were going to have a trial for me or even talk with me, or if they were just going to let me sit there and mold.

Dissatisfaction Between Black and White

I hired an English lawyer, and he went up to the District Court and talked with the District Attorney. He came back and said, "Elijah, they said to me today, that they didn't intend to have a trial for you." I said, "Why?" He said, "All they wanted to do was get you here behind the wall. They were satisfied just to put you behind the wall. They didn't care anything about bringing you to trial." So, I said, "Alright." I sent back to Chicago and told my followers there, to bring five thousand dollars here. I told them to get it one way or another. I told them to go out there and pick up scrap metal, pick up anything that they could sell and bring me back five thousand dollars.

I don't know if it's necessary or not, but while there, I had a vision and Master Fard Muhammad directed me. He said he hated what they had in mind to do with me; so, I thought it over. So I waited and called my wife who brought the five thousand dollars in the prison to give to the clerk so they could release me. And As soon as I was released, the lawyer had hurried over where I was and said to me and my wife, "For God sake, leave the city, they're planning to get you tonight."

He said, "They didn't want to see you out on a bond." And quickly, here came some white fellows asking and inquiring as what was I going to do next: Was I going out tonight or was I going to stay over? They being the enemy, I asked, "What do you want to know that for?" That evening, not that night, but that evening, I rode a Pennsylvania train, Limited, to Chicago, and it arrived the next morning around seven or eight o'clock. I was kind of relieved that I was out of all of that.

I wasn't afraid so much, because I hadn't done anything to be afraid for. Even those who arrested me said the same thing. They said, "No, you haven't done anything, but the President wants you out of the public." So, when I did do time as before mentioned, in Milan, Michigan, and I stayed there several months and years. I tried to eat the food that they manufactured, but actually they wanted to force Muslims to eat pig, not by asking us to eat it, but by forcing us to eat it, which I thought was pretty bad, because their own Bible teaches against it. Now, here you have Christians boasting and teaching the eating of that which they are divinely forbidden to eat. I thought it was terrible. I didn't say anything, because I was in jail. In prison, why should I talk when it was their property. I knew this was coming. I knew I was going through this before I went.

I want you to remember this, let us repeat what we said earlier: We do not want to bring about trouble; it's those who make trouble with us and then accuse us of causing the trouble that they have made.

Let us go in our little book, wherein [Jesus] and the scholars had a picture of a lamb drinking water down a stream and a wolf drinking water up the stream. The wolf pushed the little lamb down the stream and said, "It was you and your father that did me a great disservice." He [lamb] said, "It could not have been me, because I was not here a year ago." So the wolf said, "Well, it was your fathers then. The lamb said, "I don't even know them." Well anyway, the wolf said, "There's no need of putting up any excuse, I'm going to eat you and eventually eat them all." So, there was no way out for the lamb, even if he was innocent, he still was a victim and was accused by the wolf. The wolf was going to make some excuse for eating that innocent lamb, whether or not it had an excuse.

There are quite a few thousand of my followers over the country. I don't boast; there is no need to. We number hundreds of millions and billions over the earth; I don't need to boast of having followers. I simple am satisfied that those that see the light, accepts the truth. Time and again throughout the country where my followers are, these people, like the wolf, provoke them to do something so they'll have an excuse for killing them.

For thirty-seven long years, soon it will be forty; I have been covering the country of America with truth, not with aggression, but with truth. That is what I have been covering the country with. Now as you know it has emerged over the border. He's over there in Mexico killing us; yet, we have a little fire started over there. As well, you can find us down in Central America, where there is much trouble brewing. It's on some of the British Isles of people who speak Islam from the beginning. We actually have a record where England used to take up Muslims long time ago in planes then drop them back out on the Earth.

12 Dissatisfaction Between Black and White

One Hundred Percent Dissatisfied

Dissatisfaction is our subject here between black and white; for the world has become full of it. The world has come to a point whereas it's going to explode. The poor black man in America is blind to this knowledge, and dead to even hear it. I have been appointed by God himself, to try and take you out the way of Satan. I don't want to boast that you actually have been given to me. No one wanted you. No one wants you now, except God and myself. By my Allah, with His Power and backing, I intend to get you free.

If you are staying with those you're with, [slavery, suffering and death] will continue to happen; so, since you are dying, I would rather see you dead myself, and not from someone killing you. That prophecy belongs to you, and by law, you have the right to do what you want to do. I'm not begging you to accept what I am saying; I have someone who

will force you to do it. It is not me. I
don't need to. I have worked hard night
and day pleading with you. I'm referring
to black people. I've shown you the love
of a brother, as never a brother before;
yet, you have rejected me, because you
are proud.

You think that you have great friends in
white folks and you're willing to disgrace
yourself to get up beside them. Well,
you're not from him. You shouldn't try to
be his equal. You couldn't make yourself
his equal if you tried. I don't care how
proud you feel in your heart over what he
has taught you: the belief that some of
you have "made it." That isn't working.
You are not his equal, and he's not your
equal, even if you got them all together.
The only way that you can be the equal
with white folks is to go and lose yourself
or be born into their blood and flesh, and
the same with them. The only way that
they can become one of you is to be born
all over again into your flesh and blood.
This is the only way that you can become
brothers. You can't be brothers like you
are. You may love the white people, some
of them may love you, but you may have

to take a human transformation to find what you are looking for.

I want you to remember that we don't want to hold you here all afternoon. I simply want to get this point over to you. Dissatisfaction as you know today is in every heart of man. Several years ago when I was missioned by God to teach my people, thirty one years ago or so, ninety eight per cent of the population of the planet earth was dissatisfied. Ninety-eight and seven tenths were living at that time. Today it's hundred per cent; so, what shall be done?

The whole entire population of the planet earth is dissatisfied. I ask you scholars and scientists to tell me now, what must be done to bring about peace and satisfaction between man and man? My beloved people, I'm talking to the Blackman, if you see and hear what I see and hear, how can you act and talk as you are acting and talking? The white man's radio and his TV is not going to tell you of what the world is facing.

Dissatisfaction Between Black and White

A People Spoiled and Robbed

Blackman and woman, you say you are free. You put your fingers in your suspenders and fight to death. I'm not making fun. I just want to get to my people. You say you are free and that, "I'm a citizen of U.S.A.;" yet, you are running around in the streets begging for citizenship.

Civil Rights have been cast out and you're like a scared rabbit hiding in the south from a dog. You haven't got it yet. Yet, you still can do this. You then rear back and look at us as though we are crazy folks and don't know what we're doing. We've, the Muslims, have been trying to create love between blacks and be brothers with you, as you are our flesh and blood, and you deny and reject this.

I want to warn you this afternoon that there is something on the way that will not bring laughter to you. It won't give you time to make mock of that which you have mocked. It's all on the way. The scholars and scientists of white people are telling you and warning you. They look at next year as being the most dreadful year and they are right. This is why I wanted to be meeting with you today. We all see what difficulty lies ahead; it is terrible. It is so terrible until actually my nerves turn around. I want you to know that it's dreadful. We're going to have trouble in America. Due to dissatisfaction between black and white, and with the ignorance and misunderstanding of my people, who are the victims of the worst robbery of all time.

The Worst Robbery of All Time

Think about a man or let me put it like this: Think about a frog that's bitten and slapping his feet together under the chime of a rattler; just think over this. It's thinking it's happy. It's thinking the rattler is not going to poison him, but this is the way of the snake. It's creeping up on the frog all the time. I say to you my friends who are visiting, I'm not making you frogs nor am I making anyone else snakes. It is the characteristics I am referring to. If a man does not love himself and his kind, who does he love? Think over this. If I don't love you, my black brother, who do I love? Who is it for me to love? Who wants my love if I don't love self and my kind? Who wants my love? I want you to remember. White people, as I have learned, and I have it in black and white, are manufacturing arms in their brother's house. Throughout the country they are mining ore to produce guns to shoot black people. This is going on now. If you don't believe it, go and ask someone to open up their house you will find it. Even in his churches there are stacks of arms buried there; to do what, to kill Negroes. When the black brothers went out with a few carts of rocks, stones, and a few hand guns, there in Detroit, about fifty or more, a big deal was made of it and the National Guard was on it armed to the teeth. There was fighting in the city. They're still holding the so-called Negroes who were out there throwing stones. So anxious by nature to get at the black man, any little provocation will give them an excuse to use some of their deadly weapons on them. These soldiers were not satisfied with going after those they thought were involved, the came after the Temple of Islam as humbly as the atmosphere was that surrounded it. There was no one there doing any harm; yet the soldiers wanted to let that house, and those people in it know, that, "I would like you to come and fight so that I can kill you." They were not trying to find who started the trouble nor were they seeking justice in this thing. They are satisfied with just grabbing the first Negro they saw and killing him. Now white folks are worrying about what the Negro will do and what to do with the Negro. I know you are able to kill every one of them and I'm not saying that you are not able. You don't have to tolerate their little rocks and a few cans of gasoline, you have all types of weapons. They have been manufactures for years, just for this day with revolution starting. You know it's coming, not for five or ten years, but you've known this was coming ever since you had a Bible. It's there in the Bible. It's my foolish brothers and sisters who don't know the truth, don't want to accept the truth, don't want to go for themselves, don't want to feed themselves, because he loves you. He's not fighting for anything but for you to love him. That's what he's fighting for. He wants you to love him, but you can't love him and he doesn't know that. By nature you were not made to love him, but he doesn't know that.

Dissatisfaction: Something Must Be Done

Certainly we see it coming. This is why I'm out here. I want the friendship of Black men. I want the Black man to befriend the Black man. Running around seeking love and civil rights is not getting you any place. You must go along with the truth or else. You are a very wicked hearted Black man who will accept a bribe from white people to do evil against your own kind. This is terrible. We read it and we know it's the truth. We heard it taught from one to the other. Today white folks kill their "so-called brothers," so-called Negroes, Black people, for what? Is it to accept Negroes, to set Negroes free, to give Negroes equal justice? No, it's to help white judges. As long as they can find another day on the book, they'll give it to him and then add some more. You see black men sitting on the bench, and see what subject upon their own brother. They make you think you're going to get justice. What kind of a black man would do that to his own black brother? They love white folks. They love them. To their own detriment, they neglect the love for their own self and kind. The government, throughout the country, is raising Negroes for political positions up in high offices, that is, if he thinks you can do his people any good.

If he thinks you can do his people any good and deprive us of justice, he'll keep you where you are or raise you. But, if you would go with your people, ok, there you are. There's a higher place for the other fellow. They've got it written in the Holy Qur'an, that you my brothers sitting here should read. It's in the 26th chapter of the Holy Qur'an, section 3, entitled Moses and the Enchanters. It's not that they were something different. They were Israelites working with the Egyptians, and especially Pharaoh, against Israel. The way they intended to overtake Moses is to vanquish him. When the enchanter gathered, they said to Pharaoh, will there be a reward for us if we are the vanquishers? They wanted Pharaoh to give them a reward if they were able to vanquish Moses and Aaron. What did

Dissatisfaction Between Black and White

Pharaoh say, yes, and you shall certainly be of those who are near to me.

Dissatisfaction Between Black and White

Uncle Toms Worst Enemy To People

There is nothing of the truth that I teach you that you cannot find in black and white, in a book. Now do you think brothers, sisters and Ministers, that all of these rich clergy men and rich politicians get such wealth from the President, his cabinet members or from some close government official? Well, I ask you before we leave today, is it you? I want to reason with you. I really want to talk with you. I want you to remember that I often hear whispering out there in the streets about you. I don't know how you may getting this wealth and all these things, but they're talking about you, and they're not saying anything pleasing about you. They don't think that they can get anywhere until you are out of the way; this is the truth. I didn't put them up to this now. Don't say that I put them up to this, because they are not following me. They still may charge you with being with the other power that stands in the way: agents of white folks that will do anything for them, even at the expense of their own death. So Christians, attorneys, and you little congressmen and women, pardon me not little congressmen and women, but the big name congressmen and women, I want you to be careful. Don't get to happy because nothing last forever. I think that if a Black man gets into a position and accepts himself and his black kind, he should do it. If the white man wants to give you power, let him do it. I thank you, I thank you.

If you tried to execute the law of justice that we have in the office, you can easily tell him I thought you intended for me to execute the law. You cannot go out there if you are a black police man run down whites, law breakers and take them to the jail and beat their heads like you beat your own people's head. The next thing you know, you won't be on the job. Are the laws just for one people, you and your kind? What do you want with a job that carries out justice of the law upon your own people, and showing better treatment to them before you do so to your own? Now people, I don't blame the boy for talking about you like that, because you willfully and knowingly do evil against your own people.

I warn you my brothers and sisters, they are not following me, but I warn you. Be careful, because I heard them talking. They are dissatisfied. Teenage kids are dissatisfied with their leadership and want to make a change. They're not asking you to advise them. They don't want any of advice from an Uncle Tom. God is allowing them to see their worst enemy. His worst enemy is among himself. I don't say that we can make angels out of white folks. I don't say that we can get along with them in peace, I'm not saying that, but I do say that if we do our part and try to live with ourselves, be ourselves, speak among ourselves and kind, and go to our kind, it would eliminate a lot of tension. The contrary is only causing dissatisfaction.

You go every day and night looking to the white man for good. And then ask him to give you respect. Do you want the white race to know that you are too lazy to go for self, to do for self? Do you want them to know that you don't want to accept the responsibility of self? This is what you are telling them. If they kick you all the way down to the City Hall, what can you say: respect me? You lay down in the way, trying to force him to respect you after you refuse to do for yourself even after the Good News, which you never expected would come to you. You still insist on following the white man.

Allah (God) Offers You The Kingdom

We want to now give you the Kingdom. He offers you the Kingdom. He offers it to you. He offers you Paradise while you live, which is money, good homes, and friendship in all walks of life. I say that is good news. When He met me, I had a mixed matched coat and pants. Think over that. They were not new. My shoes had lost one side of the heel and I had a wife and six kids. Everything I got went directly to them. When I met Allah, Master Fard Muhammad, He said, "Come follow me; follow me Elijah. I don't want you to do anything but help me. Forget about where you want to go. Help me put my people and your people on top of civilization." I said, "Yes sir, I will do it. If it cost my life, I will give that and warn my people." He said, "I will back you up. Fear not, because I am with you, and there will be nothing that will come to you without my permission." He took me in. He changed my clothes. He put money in my pocket wherein there was only dust.

I want to tell you something black brothers and sisters; I didn't do anything but study and tried to show you what he had shown me: money, good homes, and friendship in all walks of life. He gave me a good home. When I moved in Chicago, I had a good home. I have a home there valued at One Hundred Thousand Dollars. This is what he gave me. I have another home in Washington DC. I have another one here in Phoenix. In Chicago, I have nineteen rooms there in one house. I also have other houses and not one time have I said to you, "Come give me something to buy me this and buy me that, never. All that I've received from you, you gave it to me free from your hearts without me asking you for it. He promises us money, good homes, and friendship in all walks of life. I had many good homes and lots of friendship. I also have transportation.

When you met me and when they found me, I had none. I was walking from Wabash to 3480 Halsted Street in Chicago to teach three times a week: Wednesdays, Fridays and on Sunday afternoon. I didn't ask anybody to give me a nickel for car fare. I was too glad to tell them the good news. It didn't make me any difference. I was glad to walk the street and talk about it. Now today, He doesn't let me suffer. I was promised keys to the Kingdom. Sometimes I fed 25 to 35 people in my dining room here or there and I still had food left. I never cared about who came and ate. There have been many white people who have sat down at my table. I enjoyed having them, because they ate and talked. I know them, they know me. Since I met with God, I've been satisfied every since. I rely on Him, Master Fard Muhammad, and I put all of my trust in Him.

Today I walk through the valley of the shadow of death, but I don't fear, because if God, Who has nurtured and raised me up in your midst to lead you out of hell doesn't protect me, who can? I'm not going to let you go. In fact, I can't get over everything I want to tell you in one sitting. I want you to know that believing in Allah, and believing in His religion, Islam, brings you everything that is needed in life. If you believe it and carry it into practice, my proud brothers and sisters, you won't have to go down licking boots. Out of all your boot licking, you still don't have anything, because you have to still go along to get along, which in turns hurt your brother.

We have money, and we're always going to have money. He doesn't care anything about your plan to get some. But through our God, whatever is in the heavens and the earth is the property of our God, Who has a presence among us. He was predicted to come from 4,000 long years from Moses. He has come. He's with us. We don't preach that He's coming; we preach He's present.

Allah's Promise of Beneficence and Protection

Long before the Muslim world was ever created, we had plenty of money. We had homes. In fact, it was our God Who prepared a home for that people. It was our God Who let them out of the darkness and into light. It was Islam. When they were savage beast in the darkness of the caves, with foreign bodies, it was our God, by the hand of His prophets, Who pulled them out. You have all but destroyed us. You have changed our color. You have changed our language. You have changed our religion. You have also changed our names. We have nothing of our own. What we have has all come from the slave-master, and their slave children intend to keep them in their names for what; so that they can go to hell with them. That is what they want. They want you called by their names and they see it in the Bible as you see. Everyone who is called by their name goes down with them. Everybody that is called by the name of Allah, who has ninety-nine, will be gathered together, defended and protected by Allah and by His armies of righteous. They are men.

"Elijah, who do you have on your side to protect us if we join on with you?" I have God Who is sufficient. I don't need anybody else. With Him, I have every dark and brown man on the earth. Whether they are Muslims or not. The yellow, brown, or red man is with the black all over the planet to get you or kill you. It's one or the other. It can't be anything else; it's either life or death.

A Mighty Great Kingdom Is On The Way

You don't know, because you are happy under the shadow of your slave-master's children. The white man has said to you and me, that we are free. Let us then go free. You are already free. Go on. You say, "Well, I don't have anything to go with." Go with God.

All who followed Moses out of the land of Egypt, Pharaoh and their cruel enemy and consistent effort of trying to make a mockery of God and Moses, they did not perish. Even in the desert, they didn't perish according to the history. God even protected them in the desert, where it looked like it was impossible; yet, it was not impossible for God. He made the heavens and the earth out of impossible.

Unity Is Key For The Blackman

I'm not going to stand up here and tell you that I want unity and love with everybody like you do, because everybody would include my enemy. You're so good that you love everybody, and yet don't love yourself. I don't want to be that type of man that loves everybody, when I can't even love myself. I don't even love my kind. So I say to you my brothers, let's move. Let's get going. We are free. Why should we fight and run after being with your slave master? Why will you pass his house up to live next to him? Why don't you get out of his house? He said you are free. He's kicking you up and down the street, siccing his dogs on you, watering you down with his hose, and you're running to his brother crying about what he has done this to you and can't he do something about it. They both are brothers. They say to themselves, you're not a brother. They don't want you. They have already let you go. To you my beloved black people here this afternoon, I want you and me to unite as one brotherhood on this planet earth, then you will get what you're asking for.

Who wants to give you something while running around like a dog, grinning in boss' face telling him that you saw a nigger pass down the block there, and if you want me to do so, I'll go get him. This is the man that is an enemy to his own people and knows people don't want him. Even the white people don't want him, but if he go catches the game the slave-master requests, then he gets bold. That's the way it happened in slavery time and its going on now among ignorant people. I say to you, I want unity among black people. Let us unite and do something for ourselves. Stop begging and angering white folks, after they have given you freedom to go for yourself. If you want to act intelligent, do as I am doing, ask the white man to help you go over somewhere. If you turn me down, I'm not surprised. Yet, I thought I'd ask since I gave you all my labor. If you don't help, I'm going, because I can't get along with you in peace. Dissatisfaction is growing into a flame of anger. Let's get together and do something for self.

Short History of The Cause of Dissatisfaction

Dissatisfaction started 6,000 years ago in the Garden of Paradise where there once was peace, but the peace breakers got in there, who was the father of these white people. They started trouble in Paradise. There book teaches you that. They had to be cast out and walked into what we call the cave sides and hills of Europe; yet, they don't deny their history. I'm not saying this for mockery. I'm only telling you this black man, because you didn't suffer what they suffered. Why join on to them to make more trouble.

They got hell 6,000 years ago. We drove them over the hot sandy desert and many of them died trying to cross. The walked until they landed in West Asia, as it was called at that time, so God taught me. They had no shoes. They were bare footed. They hardly had a string or apron to put on. All of these things came upon them for causing war in Paradise in those days. Hoping that they would die out there in the desert, they didn't, because they were destined to rule; therefore, God wouldn't let them die. I say to you, my beloved brother of the black people here this afternoon, this is the white race. They walked out of Arabia, over the Arab desert into the caves there in the hills and cave sides out in the worst part civilization, over 2,000 years. Look at what happened to them? They came up out of the caves at the call of Moses and began conquering.

They went back to those who once tied them up and started tying them up, because it was there time to rule. But today their rule is up. They could not stop it if they wanted to. They have prepared a terrible destruction. The Scientist of Islam has also prepared terrible destruction. They are not making guns, the kind that you're making. They are not building fleets of ships; not the kind that you build. They don't have to build a sky full of planes. They built one. That's enough. The white man has recognized that plane. He knows it's up there and is trying to reach it, but he can't reach it. He'd challenge it if he could reach it, but it would just be like jumping off the top of rooftop into the fire. They are prepared to destroy this world. You think that you are prepared to destroy them, and if you can't do that, you say, "Let me take revenge on the so-called Negroes and kill them." This is what you are trying to do. If there was no God for the Negro, you would kill every one of them. You have no heart or mercy. By nature, you are made without any. I don't look for you to have a heart or mercy. I would be looking for more than what nature gave you. God has taught me. And I'm not going around picking on you just because I know that. I know the nature of you, so why should I pick on you. I don't want to do that. It was my people who made you. You knew the truth was coming. It's there in the book, which all of us can read. You agreed with God, when he said He would keep you here until the day of resurrection, until the truth is made known to them, and that you would make us all deviate and take us to hell; yet, I say you were not lucky enough to get us all. Some of us will believe. Those who believe will be protected, against all of your plans. You cannot bother those who believe.

White Race's Identity Exposed

I want you, my black brothers and sisters to know that there is salvation for you today, if you will accept it. However, you need to know that this God is independent. He doesn't need you. He's not pleading to you to come to Him. He doesn't care anything about me or you, if we don't care for Him. He has said, take it or let it alone. He gave the father of the white race 6,000 years, when he pleaded to him, to not to expose him, until the day of resurrection, or when the truth is made known. He said go, this is a respite for a day. Whoever believes in you or follow you, I will fill hell with you both. This is what the enemy knows. If he can get you to follow him, you will get what's coming to you. Black man and woman, this place is not your place. Hell was not made for you. There never would have been a hell, if there had not been a man made of sin. The only way to get rid of a man made of sin, total sin, if you're not going to graft him back, is to burn him up. I'm not making fun; I'm only telling the truth. I want you to know the truth.

My father agreed to hide you until the day of resurrection. Now you're running around talking about somebody's teaching hate. I would be only a chump trying to teach hate. I can't teach hate. I don't know how. I'm just teaching truth; you say its hate. For all my life and all my past, you have not only taught us to hate ourselves, but tell us to our face that you hate us too. Being called black and ugly every since I was born; I hear that coming from white people's mouth. Now, however, you have been made manifest by He, whom your book teaches, will manifest you. You say they're teaching hate, hatred of white folks. If God doesn't like you, and I'm of God and the friend of God, what do you expect from me? Are you asking me to jump into a lake of fire, now after having the knowledge of you? No. I'm going to try to run from you. If you chase me, behind you will be my God chasing you.

Whites Are Natural Peace Breaker

Dissatisfaction has not just starting today. Dissatisfaction been here every since the people who made dissatisfaction between peoples were put on the planet. We never had any dissatisfaction between black people like this before the making of white people. If we read the history of white people Mr. Tom; well, I don't know if whether you're in here or not, Mr. Tom. The boys call you boot-lickers, some of them, Uncle Tom. So, if these things were to happen Uncle Tom, I just want to tell you that we're only trying to bring about truth, love and unity, and want you to know fairly what is here. We've been living with white people for 6,000 years. It doesn't mean that we can't live among them or away from them, but we would like to know who they are, since they can't get along with themselves in peace. How can white people set up a government of peace for the people of righteousness, when they are not at peace with each other? This is an example. All over the earth today, the

majority of white people, about four hundred million, are trouble makers. They only talk about making peace.
The War of Vietnam

If a man breaks the door down and starts shooting at us, is he the one who broke the peace? Of course he is. If I fight with that man and kill him, what am I fighting for? I am fighting to preserve the peace in my home. Am I right and justified? Another question is who sent the man in here in the first place? I could have been no one. He may have just been scared that you were preparing to harm him, so he didn't want to wait for you to come out and get him. He thought he'd be smart and come after you first. This is the way the war started in Vietnam.

Not one Vietnamese person came across the ocean and attacked America. America is not bordering her shoulders or is surrounded by foreign nations; yet, America is eight or nine thousand miles away from Vietnam's shore, fighting people in their home and then tells you and me, we should go over there and help kill these people; for what? Who sent you over there?

They're taking this one man [Muhammad Ali, seated on stage], parading him over the country, and talking about he's refusing to go to war. That wasn't it. That wasn't it and you know it. What do they care about this one man going to war? He is not going to win it for them, but stopped all other Negroes from seeing that. They think the others would give him any sympathy for his good Muslim act. The white man says, "I don't want any Muslims in our country. We don't want any righteous people here. We just want them to reject righteous and be hell raisers; anything but right. They then will be our friends." This man was attack worse than any so-called American Negro you saw in your life. Do you think some of what he was making in the ring may do the teachings of Islam some good? They even said these things. "I don't want it to help Elijah." What have Elijah done to you white folks?

We Can Not Live In Peace

Not one time can you say to Elijah, out of 37 years, that he took his followers and went to you to fight you; not one time. But you have attacked us without us even attacking you or even fighting back. You have even killed some of us, and for what, to provoke us, so we can do something for you to then justify killing all of us. That's what you want, but you won't kill all of us; I don't think so. Even if you try, you won't kill all of us. We're not forsaken today. No. We have the power of the Nations on our side, and when you start killing us, you're going to soon feel it. They've been waiting for that. We don't care though, even Elijah, I don't care anything about what God do with me. I have delivered the truth. My people don't want to believe it or follow it, but that's ok. That's all I can do. He said to me, "If they don't believe it, you come on, Elijah, you have the key. Come on and bring it back to me and you and I will go."

Dissatisfaction Between Black and White

I don't know how I was going to escape, because I rely only on His power; for I surely don't carry any weapons and I pick no fights with anyone. My followers throughout the country have been attacked. Why, because they are my follower. You are constantly trying to put all my black people against us. You way to my followers everywhere, "If you go over there, you won't be given any consideration. You know, we can't give you this job. You can't stay on this job and be a sympathizer with Elijah and his teachings, he teaches hate." I say to you my friends, black people, don't let that frighten you. This is to try you; that's all it is. We are here, and we work for our living and want you to give us a job, but they are trying you. If they don't give us a job, that's up to them. We can pack up and go. We have a home in other than America. "You say, "Well, get out and go then, I want to ask you who was living here before you started calling this your home? You can't order people out of a house that's not yours. Soon all shall understand. I'm not trying to provoke you, I'm only telling the truth to wake this black man up. Besides me, all, and especially you, have put them asleep.

He's scared to death, and I just want to let him know that he doesn't have anything to be scared of, because the earth belongs to the black people. I am asking for a home here for our people. If I was granted a home here and my people, you would live a little longer, but if we leave, you will leave.

The Filth That Filth Produces

As I have put on the last page of our paper, The Muhammad Speaks, I'm almost begging you in words there, to give us a place somewhere else other than among you, instead of in your houses, on your blocks where you don't want us. Why not? You have a house big enough to moved us out of where we are and help us get a start in another area.

My black brothers are the majority in Africa, but my ignorant brother said he doesn't want to go there. Well, you brought him out of Africa. You dumped him in America. Now, he doesn't want to go out to a place where he can be to himself, to his own with help there, until he is able to go for himself and lessen the load on you.

We know we're not going to be able to get along, because God is bringing about confusion. He's not going to let you and the black man get along. He's bringing about dissatisfaction, misunderstanding, and corruption between the people that He wants to separate; like He did Egypt. He's doing America the same way. America is so bent upon taking her Negro slave to hell with her, that she will even suffer these mean comments.

America, through her television, radio, movies, [and especially the internet] programs their girls to pull their dresses up to their waist. He constantly parades his white girls, his wives and daughters before the Negro through every type of commercial he can manufacture, from selling tooth paste to phone sex and then tell him to respect them. The white man will shoot the Negro down like a dog if he takes one of the white girls by force. This is terrible.

The white man will strip a woman and a girl and go stand them in the front of a man, and tell him don't look like you want her, when by nature, that is in the man's nature. If you go strip a female before them, naturally they can't sit there without attacking her. They'll do this to get a chance to kill more Negroes. I want you, black man, to pay no attention to them. Let them go ahead and they won't be sitting around you very long, because you're the only man they're after. They are not after their own kind; they're after you.

White Christian America, think over that, white Christian America has nothing righteous about, with their nudist form of dressing walking up and down the street. I have imagined many times, what did their pastors think when he got up on the speaker stand and looked down upon girls sitting under him with dresses half way up their thighs. How could he preach the gospel? The white people, especially England and America, is suppose to be the guide to all the races on the Earth, because they are the rulers. Now, the Baptist themselves are in such filth. Who wants to follow you? No one can hardly walk the streets without looking at half nude women; then you say you want to save your civilization, for what; to disgrace yourself and others?

I say to you, a great amount of filth is becoming the primary order of the day; think over these things. It will become so filthy, even worse than Sodom and Gomorrah's people. It will be worse than the people of Noah. Women will be going after women. Men will be going after men, boys going after boys, and girls going after girls. What should be done with a people like this? Misleading the people off the natural way and promoting the unnatural way all over the country. They lost the natural way, rather have an unnatural nature. What do you think God's going do for you? If the Bible teaches you that the people became so filthy, so evil, that God resented whoever made man; think over that. Their filthy ways stunk in the nostril of God. What do you think you are doing? What do you think He smells from you? He never smelt the filth that you spilling out to Him. If that Sodom and Gomorrah's people stunk in the nostrils of God in those days, how do you think you smell?

Today you have little babies shaking themselves before TV who are two and three years old. They are teaching their babies filth and evil from the cradle. You black fathers and black mothers who follow their ways should be beaten yourself. Any black woman and black man who looks at their child, who is from themselves, going down to the lowest form of filth and you clap and laugh at them and encourage them to do these things, you're not fit to have the child, nor fit to be a member in your Nation.

I have two granddaughters in here and they are just as afraid to put on a knee high dress before grandpa as they are to go put a rattle snake around their neck. I don't know; I would loose my mind. I don't believe I could keep control of myself. I don't think I would whip them, but I think I would go pretty close. I won't hurt the child, they are my future. I can't stand to look around and see my daughter or my granddaughter with a knee dress on.

White woman, think over how filthy you are when you sit down. Think over how filthy you look to your child down there at your knees. What do you think she or he is going to do when they get as old as you? That is if they live to do so. It's a shame. You, black woman, say well, "White folks are doing it." You are not white. White people went nude for 2,000 years only wearing the hide of animals. White people are in nudist colonies in this country. You've got no right to follow them, but you want to do that. You want them to take you as their companions. You say, "I'll do everything you do." You are a fool.

I say this to you, I know you don't like it, but I have to say it. Any black man, brown man or any one of you who allows your wives and daughters to walk out with no clothes on or come in your door with dresses above their knees, or if you permit it in with your homes, you should not say a word. If your daughter and wife wears dresses above their knees and some man grabs her and rapes her, what should or could you say? You can't say anything, because you put her out there trying to tempt him.

My brothers, my black sisters, I say to you, you are not white folks. You're supposed to act more descent than they. They actually don't care themselves. You should care, because there is nowhere in history where there ever was civilization where the people would go around half nude. We however have savages in the jungle who are not considered the equal of civilized people.

The Shame of Integration

As I conclude here this afternoon, I want to talk to the black people. I want black people to love black people. This is what you should do for yourselves: Don't be a fooled when you say to me, "The book says that we should love everybody." Then why have not you been beating the hell out of white people for four hundred years returning the "love" they have been showing you?

Why have not you been showing that you are so good a Christian as well – "loving everybody." Why didn't you go and make others love you then? I am most certain that if you ever meet God he'll say, "No nigger, I don't love you, because you love white folks." The book teaches you that, those of you who mix with white people, marry them, and run after their girls and boys. It's there in the back of your book in Revelations.

My friends, I say to you, lets wake up. We have this chance to love each other.

Let's go and love each other. If we got no chance to love each other, let's go kill each other, because we're not going any place. Nobody else wants us.

What is Islam, Christian and Muslim

You never take time to learn what Islam is. Islam is an Arab word, meaning a religion of entire submission to the will of God. A religion that challenges every principle or practice or I should first say, it carries every law, and every rule necessity for man to obey and carry into practice the way he may be successful. The religion of Islam has got everything in it that will lead you to a state of absolutely heaven. It's a religion of the Muslims. Muslim means one who has submitted to God forever in righteousness.

We have white people that call themselves Muslims and they practice Islam here in the United States and in Europe. I'm not criticizing their faith. Some of them actually believe, but by nature, they are not real Muslims. Nevertheless, God gives them credit for their faith. They won't be destroyed as you may think, but it will be you the black man of America who call yourself a Christian and a Christian Preacher. You can't be a Christian unless you are with white folks.

Christians are not black people. That's a made religion by the white man to trap black people and take them into slavery with him. There isn't no such thing as a hereafter after you are dead. That's all misunderstood. The white theologians and scientist didn't actually mean it like that, but they didn't mean to make it clear to you either. Actually, they know that after you are dead you are absolutely going back to the earth, but they also know that you can be dead another way, which is spiritually, wherein God would have to resurrect you on the day of resurrection. However, you would have to be a member of the God for Him to resurrect you and give you a chance to come with Him. Otherwise, He'll burn you with all the other of His enemies. This is the time now we're in. I want you black people to get along in peace and live like brothers.

Building In Phoenix

Dissatisfaction Between Black and White

I'm not going to charge white people with your foolish acts. They know you, but you don't know them. I want you to know both, from teachings of what God has taught me. I want you to know yourself and I want you to know them, who are other than yourselves. That doesn't mean I'm telling you to take a gun and go over there and shoot in that man's house. Do nothing to any one that you would not have done to yourself.

I have been here and have been teaching and trying to build in this beautiful city that I have made my home. My followers are helping me who in turn will help you refine Phoenix and not make Phoenix ugly, but make Phoenix beautiful. We have planned, as a token, ten houses out here in the 3200 block, and when they are built, you will find them to be very nice homes that even you who have homes, would not mind staying in one of them. This is just to show you that God has promised us good homes, money and good friendship in all walks of life. That doesn't mean that we are millionaires. We're not millionaires. We don't have enough money.

We're contemplating a 5 million dollar building in Chicago. We have gone to work on some of this, but we have a 5 million dollar plan for next year. Approximately one million dollars is going to farming. This year I am hopeful that we are going on here. I've got a white agent there as a contractor to construct and build for us. He seems to be a very fine man. He appears to be very nice and he doesn't seem to me like he wants to see if he can stick us up and rob us.

A Prey Among Wolves

It is real evil to rob a slave his whole life; when in fact, his whole life has been for you; think over that. You robbed the poor so-called Negro all his life for every dollar you could get out of him. You would cheat and rob him even though he has been your servant all his life. You have not offered him anything to go for himself, but if he gets anything, you'll get around and take it away from him, even if you have to kill him. In the South, they shoot farmers out there if his crops look better than theirs. They'll actually take it away from him. I saw that in my boyhood days. Now, you say that's someone who is teaching hate. What do you call that then? They didn't even have knowledge of your identity. They didn't care about your identity. And now you're killing them and have been killing them all your life. Just think over this: with just a little hit resistance, and you run and grab guns. You don't care if the man has anything or if he even have two arms; if he's black, shoot him. He just thinks you're a black servant and wish to kill him anytime you can find an excuse, and if there is no excuse and nobody's looking, you kill him anyway. You are a mean people. I hope God will help us and I hope He gives you what belongs to you.

We have made the greatest attempt that we possibly could for the last 400 years in this country to please you. Yet, time has manifested that there is no way to please you. Now that God has taught us who we are and who you are, we see now that it is useless. We can't please them. I tried to start my followers building; yet, you seek to charge us for everything you possibly can to rob us if you think we have any money. You seek to take it away from them. This is an evil mind, which is going to lead you to that which you would not want to be led to. God is well able to punish you and take what you have and give it to who He pleases. That is what the Bible is telling you. God has taken the Kingdom from whom He pleases and gives it to who He Pleases. He's not lacking in power force.

War Within And War Without

You're not so powerful, just because you're going up above the skies, that you think you can whip God. He made the clouds and He made that which you are trying to live on and He made you. I don't see why you would act so proud, dishonoring your father and your mother like that. Nobody up there needs to come and attack the earth from the moon. They're not going to do that. They're going to use what's in the atmosphere of the earth and what's in the earth to destroy what's on the earth. I have been taught how it's going to be done and it can be done just like that. You don't have anything to destroy the people of this earth before they destroy you. I Don't boast that. I want you black brothers to know this: that the white race is not going to destroy everybody on the earth. If they go to fighting right now, they're not going to even get very far, because everybody's sitting and watching them to start, to in turn justify their start. I'm not boasting, but I warn you of the tense situation that is bound to explode within a few months. We're not going to attack you, but don't be dreaming that we don't need to. We're not going to do it; yet, you hate us for teaching the truth worse than you hate all of those that try attacking you. You hate us worse and we know that. If I was in your position, I would too; that is, if it was me, not if I were you. I would act like you. Now, if it were me, I would exercise a little more judgment on the thing.

Better to understanding how not to get myself caught up in the trap so that I'm trapped by my trap. If I set the trap good and if the hunted looks like it wants to go in, I would leave the trap. If it wants more bait put in it, I'll throw some more bait, but I won't go in. Now, you're thinking about how you're going to kill Negroes next year. This is what you're thinking. And I hear that you are thinking about killing all the Muslims when you get started. You have every white family and every white home armed for them to shoot every Negro they see. This is what has been told to me. I repeat, you have every white family and every white home armed for them to shoot every Negro they see.

Some of your white friends told me about them. I didn't know it. I want to tell you one thing like this: You can get yourself destroyed, because the people who will come against them, you will not be able to destroy. They are ready to destroy you and have been ready for seventy long years. Think over seventy long years, not seven years, but seventy long years. They planned your whole downfall in Vietnam and you know you can't win. They intended keeping you there; for what, to burn you out. You can't whip China. China's well prepared for you and was prepared a half a century ago for you. You can't win. They would let you beat up a hundred or two million people in order to get you weakened.

You can't force Russia to meet in a friendship with you to get their goods, because God made him your enemy. He's going to do what God bid him to do. It's you; you are the trouble maker. You are the enemy of all people of the earth, even against yourself, and they're proud. And you think that your power and your wealth will defend you, can they?

Nebuchadnezzar and Belshazzar were examples; both of them went down. The people of Noah boast that they were something; they went down. The people of Sodom and Gomorrah thought they were something, but they went down early that morning before the sun could get up good; they were gone. They come out trying to attack God's people, which is all God would need for them to do; so, He would have a good reason for killing them. Pharaoh also thought he would be a big man. He told one of his engineers to build him a building that he may reach the God of Moses. Now, there was no such thing as Moses telling them his God was up in the sky some place. This is talking about today. You are trying to reach the God of Elijah and the Muslims today up there in the sky.

I know you have heard that there are people up there. They are up there, but you can't get to them. They're going to do their work. The ship of Noah was a sign, because that boat saved Noah and his followers on top of that water, that raging water. So shall a ship in the sky save the righteous in the last days.

Educate Your Own Children

We want schools, my dear black brothers and sisters. We want schools to ourselves. Why should we want to send our children among the children of our enemy, who will be taught and trained to hate each other, to fight each other, to do every kind of nasty thing? Why do we want that, when the white man is offering you a school to yourself? He will give you one. He doesn't want you. He knows you are causing him trouble, and eventually he will get you out of the way; don't worry. We know that's coming. He'll get you out from among him very soon. This is the way Pharaoh kept on until finally he had to let them go. He started off fighting. I say to you my friends, don't let Pharaoh and his magicians deceive you. Again, I want to ask you, why can't we get together and build a school house, college or anything we want for our children? Why can't we do these things? If we are together we can. We have had schools to ourselves and have not had any trouble for many years. We have teachers their today who are very fine teachers; some with Doctorate degrees. We don't hire teachers unless they have a college degree to teach our children. We have to hire educators. You educators, teachers and black folks in mixed schools, why don't you come on and take your children to a school to themselves? They will learn more. Why not ask the government to give you a school to yourselves? You say that's segregating. Segregating? No, it's separating. Should not you want to be separated? Should not you want to be separated from your slave- masters, who mistreated you over the past three or four hundred years, and are still doing it?

White Race Are The Murderers of Prophets

Nobody wants an American Christian Negro. The white people don't even want that, because they're not good Christians. That's right. They preach Christianity, but they're not Christian. Christian means one in God and especially in Christ who they look forward to come in the last day. The Christ, the Anointed One, or the Son of Man, they're not with him. They are ready to go to war against that man. They're doing that now. They don't want to see no coming of Christ. The Bible teach in revelations: They saw Him coming in the nation with anger. If they were good people, they would be happy, but they're angry, because that upsets their world. They don't want no Christ. They don't want no Son of Man. They don't want a Jesus. They killed him when he was here before. If another one like him came, they will kill him. They would kill all the prophets. I mean white people. Their race either killed the prophets of God or put them in prison, or laid them away in dungeons. All this was done by white folks, not black people. These prophets of God could never stay long among white people; why, because the white people themselves are the devil, and the devil doesn't need a prophet, that's right. The prophets made no progress among devils trying to preach righteous, because by nature, he is against righteous. My friend, I'm sorry I have to tell you this though. I want to be sure you don't come up one day soon and say, "Well, if you had told us we would have understood;" so, now you won't have that excuse. I tell you plainly to your face, and if you want it, take it and if you don't want it, leave it. I have accomplished my job.

Prepare Yourself For The Day of Want

We are trying to raise a million and a half dollars, which is going towards food for black people. You're going to have a famine in this country, and I mean a famine. You don't know what you are doing while around here drinking whisky, beer, playing cards, shooting dice, running up and down the street looking for sweet hearts. You don't know what it's all about, but I'm telling you, you will soon see. It's not going to be years away. You will see it soon. I'm just a few days ahead of you. I warn you. I know you. You call everybody a liar except white folks, but you won't be able to make Elijah out of a liar, because I gave you what God gave me. Pretty soon, pretty soon, I say, fly to Allah, your God and to your people and my people. White people have done very little since you have been out of slavery, I think so. He did very well to have mistreated you, but still, they have done very well trying to educate you since you've been out of slavery. They are giving you jobs to work for money. They never object to you buying fine clothes. They sell them to you. Whenever you have money to buy, they sell it to you. I don't say that they were so bad to you after all. They would give you hell naturally, because you asked for it, this is the truth.

Respect of Intelligence and Authority

You don't have the knowledge of how to respect people. You don't want to respect people of intelligence and authority. You have to learn to respect people of authority. You may get along with them better. What would I, Elijah, and my followers look like leaving out of here this evening and say we're not going to pay attention to the authorities of Phoenix? I'm asking for trouble. No, this is none of our homes; so, we bought homes and yet if for some reason it comes to not being ours, whereas the Phoenix authorities want that little home at 2122 east Violet Drive, he can take it, and Elijah will look for another one. This is right. I'm only telling you how much authority they have. I want you to remember that you can't bully the white man, telling them to do this and that and they do it. They know you're going get the worse end of it. If you act intelligent and show respect to authority, by nature, we are forced to give respect to those who give respect to us.

We can't go out tomorrow morning and ask the white man to make and give you a job, and if he refuses, you curse him out. Or fight the white man for the job, then get on the job and sit down on him. This is the way of a fool. You can't charge that to the white man. You can't tell him that you want a job, to show you where he wants you to work and then go there to sit down. He didn't send for you or pay you to sit down. If he did, you could have just stayed home and he would have sent you a check there. That makes no sense. Respect people. Don't walk around the foreman taking to him like a common person like yourself or like another laborer. He is higher ranking than you. Respect the superintendant. He is the higher authority than the foreman. Respect the faculty folks. Respect the office manager. Respect the faculty owners. Respect everybody who is in authority over you, black or white. Submit to them and respect them. Do not go around trying to be independent and bossy when you don't have anything. My friend, humble yourself so that you can master yourself. People will show you their love and respect. Nobody wants such a people as that. I'm only telling you these things, because I know pretty soon, pretty soon, all I can say pretty soon, you will remember these things. I'm probably not going to teach here anymore and you will remember these things. You all won't be in this place any more. I don't think so. If you do, it will be a surprise to me.

I want you my dear black brothers to stop putting fault on everybody else. Even as far as a rattles snake lies there in the dust, if you go there and kick on it or picking on him, if he stings you, it's your fault. Why didn't you leave him alone or go on about your business? Perhaps you go picking him up trying to put him in your pocket and you got struck. He didn't belong in your pocket. I say my friend, learn to be yourself. Do something for self and go for self. If the slave master says you are free, ask the slave master if you don't have any shoes to wear down the road, ask him to give you a pair of his. Tell him, I'm on my way boss.

Do For Self or Suffer

I want you to remember something else. We are taking our salary and our checks giving them to the white grocery man for groceries a week. Why shouldn't we get together and go out there on the earth, dig up the earth like he has done and grow something? Here you have 22 million so-called Negroes in the kitchen of the white man. They go along and eventually find themselves arguing with the cook over a t-bone steak. Why don't you go grow you a cow and get a t-bone steak from it? I'm telling you, they have plenty farms throughout the country to sell, they have beef and lamb to sell. They have everything you want to make a start for yourself. They will sell it to you, though it may be high or higher than you expect it, or higher than you think they should; don't argue, because they're not your friend. Just consider that if you got by with anything, you were lucky. If they act friendly to you and act on the high level of what we call justice, then give

them big credit.   Remember them,
because they did good for you.

I say my friends, in my conclusion, let's
do something for self.   I say to you
dissatisfaction between white and black
is going to come to an explosion point in
this old country they call America and
soon.   I have heard something along the
lines of it's going to be terrible.   It is not
the little black fellow out there who's
going to do a lot of things.   It's the white
man who has planned to do a lot of
things to the little black fellow.   This is
what I am trying to make you aware of.

Friendship In All Walks of Life

To you my beloved preachers, my father was a preacher. My grandfather was a preacher and now I am a preacher, but I'm a different preacher. I'm teaching a different religion over this earth. I have hundreds and thousands of people following me. You can go almost any place in Africa and you'll stop and will hear them say, "Yes, I know Elijah Muhammad." The first thing he wants to do is pray to Allah for Elijah Muhammad to come. They are with me. They love me. They come to me in America from Africa. Asiatic black people throughout Asia love me. I'm not boasting, because it's you that I want. You and I are one of the same. God gave you to me. I want to put a Nation on the earth with the help of God the likes of which has never seen before. Not that I would do these things by my power, but I want to get you to where the God would do it for you. He will do it if you follow me. The earth is full of everything that man can hope for.

As Thou Has Done

I say to you my friends in my conclusion, let us live together in peace. The earth is full of unrest, war making, killing, and the destruction of people on earth, on the sea, in the sea, and on every country on the earth. It's going on in the Holy Land.

I say my beloved brothers and sisters; think it over. Stop being proud of being a so-called American. Try and be proud of being who you are: something of your people and not of America. America belongs to white people, and America is all bogged down in war all over the earth, and her enemies may one day sitting on the border, then it won't be no more America. Once they ever get here, they are bound to come to her borders. They probably may stop at some point; nevertheless, America won't ever be the same anymore. They're going to drive America out of Asia and America knows it, whether she wants to come out or not. I think she wants to come out, but she's ashamed to give up without winning. She will never win. Those people have been preparing for America, England, France and all white people for over fifty years. You can't whip them, they'll make you waste all of your wealth right there in that continent, getting nowhere, and that's what they intend to do. They have been working to get her trapped so that they can strip you of your wealth, they don't mind losing a few Buddhists and Hindus over there. They don't mind you killing a few, just as long as they get you. They don't care anything about those Hindus. They're not Muslims. If you were over there killing Muslims, you would have been out a long time ago. The righteous is not to be just slaughtered like flies.

My Record of Peace

Remember a Muslim is a righteous person. He doesn't go looking over the earth for a fight. He doesn't seek to fight anywhere. He's not an aggressive person. He's a humble person. When you find a person that's aggressive and he says he a Muslim, he is not. A Muslim is a very humble person, a reasonable person, a friendly person. He just doesn't want you to take advantage of him, but he is friendly. He doesn't seek to take advantage of people. I am one myself and you have 37 years of my presence here with you. You cannot find any place in my history for the past 37 years that I have tried to do anything other than the right thing, or tried to make anything except peace with you or anybody. Just look over my history. I lived in Chicago every since 1934 and that's, to date, now 33 years there. We never caused a police attack. We don't seek that. Police attacked us once or twice and God punished them for it, like he's doing today. Every way that you attack us, God punishes you if it's nowhere but in Vietnam. Don't think you get away with it. This we all understand.

Appeal To The Intellectual and Professional Classes

So I say to you again my beloved brothers and sisters and especially to the intellectual group who may be visiting us today, we love you. We want your help. You have education. Help your people. The white people who taught you the education, they don't need you; they have their own educators. Come teach your own uneducated people. We will help you. We will pay you a salary. We are paying teachers with degrees, with doctor degree salaries. We have a few with us. We pay as much as the white schools pay them. We don't ask you to do something for us for nothing. You will find that if you want a nation, you have to go down to the bottom and build them up.

You have a good way, a good start today to build up your people; not like the white people when they came over here from being in the bushes. It had taken him a long time. Now, he has made it modern and you can start very easy. Why not start for yourself. Do something for yourself. Don't beg white people to build apartment houses when you're sitting up with the money in your pocket and could do it yourself. If you would unite and put your money together and say, "Brother, come on. Let's build our people an apartment house here. They will pay for it in the long run. Why don't we work together and act like civilized people."

We want you to know that we thank you so much for coming out here and listening to the truth and listening to the importance of uniting and doing something for self. We thank you for listening to the importance of being friends to your black selves and our black kind, instead of trying to run around and mixing our black kind or selves into white people; trying to make friends with them so we can be called white folks.

Yesterday when Uncle Tom, back in slavery time, was seen licking and lapping over the master for a little buttered biscuit and a little piece of fried chicken, we could get over that, but you are here today walking around in this modern civilization acting the same: wanting a piece of fried chicken from the boss' table, today is different.

Jesus gave it just right when he said Lazarus laid at the rich man's table. You have fulfilled that and are still fulfilling it. You see the dogs have been sicced on you and you saw yourself laying right at the gate begging. That's the fulfillment you and don't think that's somebody else, that's you.

Praises be due to Allah forever. The dissatisfaction between black and white can be easily cured by black going to black, and white going to white. That will cure all the dissatisfaction. Go to yourself. If you don't have anything to go with, ask the white man – since you gave him all your labor for free, and if he doesn't give you anything, turn to your God and people and you will get something. They will help you. They're anxious to help you if you will submit to your own. They're not going to take you with a cross hanging around your neck, but if you have the crescent, which shows some sign of intelligence, they will accept you. If a man displays the sun, moon and the star, he can claim the most intelligent things, and the most essential things of man in the stars. Everybody recognizes and respect that; yet, when you hang a cross around your neck, you are telling the people, I'm the murderer of God's prophets. The sign is around your neck says, I am one of the practitioners and worshipers of the murderers of Jesus. That's what you are telling the world, that you are the murderers Jesus. You are saying that you love those who murdered Jesus. You are saying that you love and worship those who are the murderers of the prophets.

May the peace of Allah go with you, wherever you go, if you want peace. I pray that Allah's peace will come to you.

Thank you for your patience and endurance [with these writings] and your respect of what we have to say, as I say unto you, in the Name of Allah,

As-Salaam-Alaikum.

Dissatisfaction Between Black and White

Other Titles By
Messenger Elijah Muhammad [EM] & Nasir Hakim [NH], Founder MEMPS

All Titles Below Are Softcover

Title	Price
A Plain Understanding of the Red Dragon	EM $12.95
Blood Bath	EM $6.95
Christianity Versus Islam	EM $11.95
Does Elijah Muhammad Teach True Islam	NH $14.95
Everything Was Going So Well...Then We Accepted Jesus:	EM $14.95
Exposing the New Dangers of Pork	NH $9.95
For the Black Woman	RH $14.95
History of the Nation of Islam	EM $11.95
How to Eat to Live, Book 1	EM $12.95
How to Eat to Live, Book 2	EM $13.95
How To Stop Poisoning Yourself The Pure And Natural Way	NH $18.95
Is Elijah Muhammad the Offspring of Noble Drew Ali and Marcus Garvey	NH $9.95
Message to the Blackman in America	EM $17.95
My People Are Destroyed	EM $12.95
Nations Are Destroyed Because Men Forget	NH $13.95
Our Saviour Has Arrived	EM $14.95
Religion: Who Needs It?	NH $9.95
The Divine Sayings of Elijah Muhammad Volumes 1, 2 And 3	EM $7.95
The Fall of America	EM $15.95
The Flag of Islam	EM $8.95
The Genesis Years of Elijah Muhammad	EM $24.95
The God-Science of Black Power	EM $10.95
The Mother Plane	EM $7.95
The Real ID Jack	NH $13.95
The Reality of God Forces Other Realities	NH $9.95
The Science of Time	NH $10.95
The Secrets of Freemasonry	EM $7.95

The Supreme Wisdom - Volume 2	EM $8.95
The Supreme Wisdom, Volume 1	EM $7.95
The Theology of Time	EM $18.95
The True History of Elijah Muhammad-Black Stone	EM $18.95
The True History of Jesus	EM $10.00
The True History of Master Fard Muhammad (Allah in Person)	EM $14.95
Theology of Time - Abridged Indexed by Subject	EM $24.95
They Thought They Were Followers of Elijah Muhammad	NH $13.95
We Must Preserve Our Distinction or Die!	NH $10.95
Why Must Elijah First Come?	EM $13.95
Yakub (Jacob)	EM $11.95

Hardcover Titles are available online.

For more information Call
Phone & Fax 602 466-7347

or visit:
www.memps.com
or
See Back cover for
contact information

Made in the USA
Lexington, KY
04 December 2015